Dartmouth t
A Pictorial Guide

by
Robin Rose-Price

ORCHARD PUBLICATIONS
2 Orchard Close, Chudleigh, Devon TQ13 0LR
Telephone: (01626) 852714

ISBN 1 89896469 6

Printed by
Hedgerow Print, Crediton, Devon EX17 1ES

i

Acknowledgements

A special thank you to my wife Alison who has accompanied me on the many photographic expeditions needed to complete this book and taking on more than her share of work in our business while I sat at the computer.

I would also like to thank the following for their assistance and encouragement:
The Cookworthy Museum, Kingsbridge.
The Dartmouth Museum.
The Geography Department of the Slapton Ley Field Centre.
The Salcombe Life Boat Station and the Trustees of Cliff House Salcombe.
Paul Way for the use of his family watercolour on Hallsands, page 19.
Lynn Bloomfied for her photographs on pages 23 and 25.
Humphrey Waterhouse for the use of his father's wartime photograph page 31.
David Cross for allowing the reproduction of the Battle of Blackpool Sands graphics, page 9.
The Devon Information Library for permission to reproduce watercolours by W.Payne, pages 10 and 11.
Sue Cook for information around Gara Rock and East Portlemouth.

For my grandson   Innes Rose-Price
May he follow in my footsteps and appreciate the magnificent
beauty of our coastline.

Also by the same author

400 Years in Torcross	1602 - 2002 A pictorial history of its development and of its inhabitants over the years, including the extreme weather conditions the village has faced and survived.
The Land we left Behind	A pictorial history and memories of the war years in the South Hams - the evacuation of the population and Exercise Tiger.
Torcross and Slapton Ley	A pictorial record of the geological formation and history of Slapton Ley and the village of Torcross.

Dartmouth to Salcombe

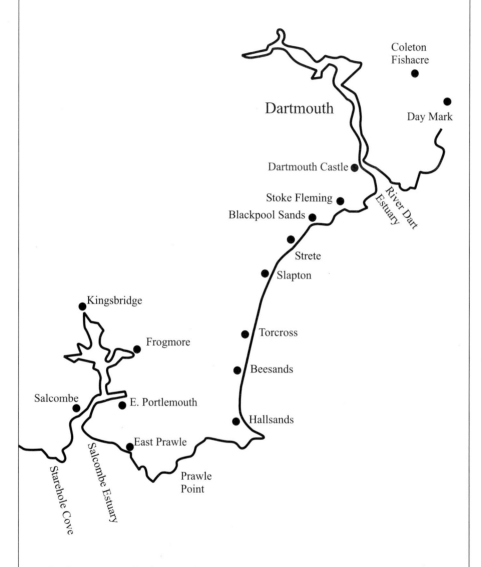

Coleton
Fishacre

Day Mark

Dartmouth

Dartmouth Castle

Stoke Fleming

Blackpool Sands

River Dart Estuary

Strete

Slapton

Kingsbridge

Frogmore

Torcross

Beesands

Salcombe

E. Portlemouth

Hallsands

East Prawle

Prawle
Point

Starehole Cove

Salcombe Estuary

Scale approx 1 inch = 3 miles

Dartmouth. One of the most exciting ways to arrive in Dartmouth is on the Lower Ferry which operates between Kingswear and Dartmouth. The two car floats are propelled across the River Dart by small tug boats named after Sir John Hawley (1340 – 1408) who was a leading merchant in the town and fourteen times Mayor of Dartmouth. They were built in 1966 by local boat builders Philip and Sons.

The boat float is the name for the inner harbour for small craft. Originally it was completely open to the River Dart on one side, but with the building of the road along the embankment, this has been reduced to a small entrance under the road.

Bayards Cove is the earliest surviving quay in Dartmouth. The houses at the southern end and the circular Bayards Cove Fort are from Tudor times, the buildings at the northern end are 18th century. A plaque here commemorates the visit of the Pilgrim Fathers in 1620. Their ships, the Mayflower and the Speedwell, were taking in water, so they berthed at Bayards Cove for repairs. Speedwell was in a such bad condition that soon after they left Dartmouth, they had to put back into Plymouth, where it was abandoned and Mayflower sailed to America on her own.

Warfleet Creek takes its name from the time it was used as a safe assembly point for over 100 ships setting out for the Second Crusade in 1147 and again for the Third Crusade in 1190. More recently it was the site of the Dartmouth Pottery which closed its doors in 2003 and was sold for redevelopment into residential units.

Dartmouth Castle dates from the 1480s and used to protect the river entrance with its cannon fire power and with the aid of a chain slung across the river-mouth to Kingswear Castle on the other side. These defences were aimed at keeping out the French, though the chain was later used to bar rival Cornish fishermen from landing their catches in Dartmouth.

Gallants Bower fortified earthwork was built by the Royalists between 1643 and 1646 during which time they held Dartmouth from the Parliamentarians. In early summer the steep earth banks of the fort are covered with bluebells and pink campions.

A walk around the ramparts of Gallants Bower gives a commanding view across the mouth of the Dart towards the World War II gun battery at Froward Point and to the Day Mark which can be seen on the top of the hill.

The Day Mark. On the Kingswear side of Dartmouth Harbour stands the Daymark stone tower. It is 24m (80ft) high and was built in 1864 as a navigational aid to assist Royal Mail ships travelling to the colonies. It made recognition of the Dart Estuary much easier to find when ships were several miles out to sea.

Coleton Fishacre. Close to the Day Mark is the National Trust house and gardens of Coleton Fishacre. The house was built between 1923-26 for Rupert D'Oyly Carte, whose father Richard had been the impresario behind the operettas of Gilbert and Sulivan. The gardens descend a narrow combe to the cliff path and to Pudcombe Cove where the family used to swim.

5

Dartmouth's Britannia Royal Naval College was built in 1902 to replace the training hulks Britannia and Hindostan which were moored on the river. In 1944 the college was used as the U.S. Navy headquarters for the overseeing of activities carried out by allied forces preparing for the D-Day landings of June of that year.

An American tank waits for provisions by Coronation Park, Dartmouth which was used as a military depot. (For more information on the D-Day preparation and of the ill fated 'Exercise Tiger' see *The Land we left behind* by Robin Rose-Price).

6

1st June 1944. Half tracks are reversed onto a L.S.T (Landing Ship Tank) ready for a quick exit when they landed on the Normandy beaches. An armada of over 480 craft left Dartmouth Harbour for the invasion.

Other more peaceful journeys also started in Dartmouth. Dartmouth Station was the only operating British Rail station in the country with no tracks running to it. Passengers from the train were met by coach and horses and taken along the coast to Torcross and Kingsbridge.

Stoke Fleming. The narrow road through the village remains much the same as in the picture but now it takes a very different type and volume of traffic.

St Peter's Church was built approximately 700 years ago. On the floor of the nave is the magnificent 14th century brass of John Corp (1361) and his grand-daughter Elynore (1391). It is the oldest dated brass in the west of England. The 1891 wooden pulpit, depicts sixty animals, beautifully carved by Miss Violet Pinwill when aged just seventeen.

George Bidder, 1806 - 1878, the mathematical genius and famous engineer is buried in the churchyard, to the south of the tower. He worked with Robert and George Stephenson on the London and Birmingham Railway and later as chief engineer on the Norwich and Lowestoft line on which he designed and introduced the first ever railway swing-bridge. However, his most important work was the construction of the Victoria Docks in London. As a mathematical genius his mental capabilities were used to great effect by Parliamentary committees in examining financial papers and intended expenditure.

Blackpool Sands is one of the most beautiful and well run beaches on the south Devon coast and is popular with old and young alike.

The Battle of Blackpool Sands 1404. A 2000 strong Breton force landed at Slapton in an attempt to capture nearby Dartmouth. As they advanced down the hill to Blackpool Valley they were faced with a flooded ditch which had been dug by the English militia under the direction of John Hawley (the Mayor of Dartmouth). As the knights on their heavily armoured horses attempted to cross they floundered in the mud, giving the advantage to the untrained local militia and the day was won.

Strete. The coach and horses would have continued along the toll road through Strete. The upkeep of the road was the responsibility of each parish through which it passed, so toll houses were strategically placed. The last house in Strete still bears the name Turnpike Cottage.

The road then dropped to down to Strete Gate, using the steep track that is now used only by pedestrians and forms part of the South West Coast Path.

Slapton Sands. Strete Undercliff is known to have existed on the beach in the vicinity of Strete Gate but there are no signs of it today. Perhaps the ruins behind the boat in the picture are those of the lost village.

The Royal Sands Hotel stood on the site now occupied by the War Memorial on the shingle ridge of Slapton Sands. It was built in 1831 and received royal status when King Edward VII stayed there in 1855. It attracted sportsmen from far and wide who came to fish for pike, rudd, perch and eels in the famous Slapton Ley.

'Exercise Tiger'. Slapton Sands was the chosen site for Exercise Tiger in April 1944. This was a full scale practice landing for D-Day. Unfortunately 600 American soldiers lost their lives at sea when their convoy came under attack during the night from German E boats. A further 200 lives were lost on the beach as a result of friendly fire. Not only was live ammunition used by the defenders to give greater realism to the exercise, but the once proud Royal Sands Hotel was reduced to rubble by Naval gunfire prior to the landing. However, there is a popular story that a stray dog caused the damage by wandering into the mine fields around the hotel.

The Evacuation of the Local Population.
In 1954 the United States Army presented the memorial in gratitude to the 3000 people who gave up there homes and farms in December 1943, with only six weeks notice prior to occupation by allied troops. The evacuated villages were Blackawton, Chillington, East Allington, Sherford, Slapton, Stokenham, Strete and Torcross.

Unfortunately the stone mason left off the name of the village of Sherford. This was not corrected until 2002 when the memorial monument was relocated to its present position following severe undermining of its foundations in the storms of the previous year.

THIS·MEMORIAL WAS·PRESENTED·BY·THE UNITED·STATES·ARMY AUTHORITIES·TO·THE PEOPLE·OF·THE·SOUTH HAMS·WHO·GENEROUSLY LEFT·THEIR·HOMES·AND THEIR·LANDS·TO·PROVIDE A·BATTLE·PRACTICE·AREA FOR·THE·SUCCESSFUL ASSAULT·IN·NORMANDY IN·JUNE·1944 THEIR·ACTION·RESULTED IN·THE·SAVING·OF·MANY HUNDREDS·OF·LIVES·AND CONTRIBUTED·IN·NO·SMALL MEASURE·TO·THE·SUCCESS OF·THE·OPERATION THE·AREA·INCLUDED·THE VILLAGES·OF·BLACKAWTON CHILLINGTON EAST ALLINGTON·SHERFORD SLAPTON·STOKENHAM STRETE·AND·TORCROSS TOGETHER·WITH·MANY OUTLYING·FARMS&HOUSES

The new memorial was unveiled in November 2002 by Major Jeffrey Nelson, representing the US Ambassador and Deputy Lord Lieutenant of Devon, Vice Admiral Sir Robert Gerken, KCB, CBE, DSC, DL. Also present were Councillor Mary Strudwick, Chairman of Devon County Council and Councillor Gordon Rothwell, Chairman of South Hams District Council.

13

Torcross Tank Memorial. In 1984 local hotelier, Ken Small, paid for this Sherman tank to be recovered from the sea bed, where it had lain since Exercise Tiger in 1944. It was placed on a raised piece of ground as a memorial to those who gave their lives in the exercise.

Four of the remaining veterans of Exercise Tiger came over from the United States to mark the 60th Anniversary in 2004 and to tell their harrowing stories to the world's media. From left to right are Richard Ferguson, Steven Sadlon, William Hicks and Louis Seibel.

Torcross was first mentioned in manorial records in 1602 when it was just a collection of fishermen's huts. With the construction of the road in 1854 the stage coach brought wealthy families on holiday from the big cities. The area grew in popularity and with the coming of the motor car many of the visitors fell in love with the village and purchased second homes.

The promenade is ideal for a leisurely amble after sampling one of the excellent eating facilities on the seafront. During the summer the beach is popular with sun bathers and swimmers as well as commercial fishing boats and all manner of water sports.

Historically the combination of spring tides and severe easterly gales, periodically caused damage to Torcross seafront. In 1978 the beach level dropped dramatically and the foundations of the houses were exposed. Boulders were placed in front of the houses to hold back the waves.

Unfortunately, four of the houses were so badly damaged that they needed the sea facing walls completetely rebuilt. The Start Bay Inn lost its cafe which was located in the pub's car park. The force of the waves even washed the pool table out of the building. In 1981 the new sea defences were completed. These consist of steel piles driven deep into the beach and a wave return wall built behind them to protect the promenade and the seafront houses in the future.

Beesands was once a thriving fishing village with most of its residents earning their living from the sea. The pub, The Cricket Inn, has been the focal point for the community since 1823. It derives its name from one of its earliest owners who was named Cricket.

Sadly, as the local fish stocks dwindled and the fishing grounds moved further and further off shore, larger boats were needed to reach them. These boats could no longer be launched in the traditional manner of pulling them up and down the beach on wooden runners, so the Beesand's fishermen had to travel to Dartmouth each day for the nearest deep water moorings. All that is left now of the once proud fleet are a few small boats with outboard motors.

The grassed area between the village of Beesands and the football pitch was once occupied by a camp site with over one hundred static caravans, a shop and a clubhouse as shown in the picture. Beesands is not a place you drive through, only to and from, and as the holiday site grew the narrow lanes could not cope with the volume of traffic. Legal battles between the site operators and the District Council lasted many years before it was confirmed to be a village green, whch heralded the exodus of holiday caravans.

Beesands has suffered the same storm damage as Torcross over the years. The new sea wall protects the old fishermen's cottages, many of which are now second homes or holiday cottages.

The old village of Hallsands. Nestled against the cliffs near Start Point, the fishing village of Hallsands survived for over 200 years. In 1895 the developers of Devonport Docks in Plymouth were given permission to remove 650,000 tons of shingle from between the high and low water marks from Tinsey Point to just south of the village. This effectively took away the natural sea defences and the village was badly damaged by storms in 1903 and again in 1917. However the government who approved the development of the dockyard refused to admit it was their fault.

The village was abandoned after the storm in 1917 with all but two of the twenty eight houses rendered unsafe. The house on the right of the picture belonged to Lizzie Ann Prettijohn, who was one of the few able to return to their homes.

Lizzie Ann Prettijohn continued to live in her house until she died in 1965. Quite naturally she considered herself the official guide of Hallsands and everyone who visited the old village was shown around by 'a proper lady of Hallsands'. If she took a liking to a visitor they would be invited in for a cup of tea. This seemed a good idea until they saw one or more of her many hens walking about amongst the dishes on her dining table!

The Trout Sisters. The Trout family was one of those unable to return to their home in the old village after the storm of 1917, but they stayed in the area and through hard graft and determination, they were eventually able to build a very successful hotel on the cliff top above the old village.

From left to right Gertrud Vogtle, Edith, Ella and Patience Trout.

Ella and Patience Trout spent much of their time fishing. The hotel guests were all expected to help haul the nets when there was a big catch. If they didn't they did not get a booking for the following year!

Sadly, after Ella and Patience died Edith tried to run the hotel on her own, but when German-born Gertrude Vogtle left to start her own business in 1959 Edith decided she had had enough of the world and locked herself away in the hotel as a recluse. She left everything in the hotel as if ready for the guests to return. The beds were made, the tables in the dining room were laid, even the fat remained in the deep fat fryer until her death in 1975. She lived most of that time without water or electricity or telephone.

In 1976 Trouts Hotel was purchased by Robin Rose-Price and his family. By this time most of the Hallsands ruins had been washed into the sea by subsequent storms. The old village was a major tourist attraction at that time, with many thousands of people wandering through the ruins during the course of a holiday season. Wilson's Rock, seen sticking out of the water on the right of the picture, was covered completely by the beach before the dredging commenced in 1895.

The year after Edith's death the hotel was coverted into holiday apartments which evolved over the next twenty years as the guests returned time and time again. A games room, swimming pool, tennis court, adventure play area and putting green were all added to keep the young families and the author's own children entertained.

Start Point Lighthouse. A light first shone from Start Point Lighthouse in 1836. The present light has a group of three flashes every ten seconds with a range of twenty five miles. The twenty five metres high tower is open to the public during the summer months.

In 1989 the cliff collapsed taking the old fog horn engine room with it. The cliff moved to within two metres of one of the keeper's houses, rendering it unsafe to be used. By 1992 the light had been automated and the last of the keepers moved out. Their homes are now let as holiday accommodation.

23

Peartree Point. On the southern side of Start Point a very exposed secion of the cliff path leads to Peartree Point, where you can sit on the grass and watch the seals basking on the rocks or even swimming close to shore to have a look at you!

Photo of seals by Tim Stanger, South West Images.

Mattiscombe Beach is the first proper sandy cove you come across after all the shingle beaches of Start Bay. It is a favourite with local people and visitors alike. Prawle Point can be seen in the distance.

At the southern end of Mattiscombe Beach are two extraordinary earth pillars, standing on sections of more residual rock which protects them from damage by wave action. They were once attached to the land behind them as small headlands. On top of each pillar is a head deposit of harder rock, which has protected them from weather erosion (a bit like an umbrella).

Lannacombe Beach. The house next to the car park was once a corn mill and the grinding stones can still be seen lying in the grass beside the road. The wave cut platform which rises out of the beach was formed during the inter-glacial period about 120,000 years ago, when the sea level was much higher. The brown layer above the wave cut platform was deposited by the combined action of ice, water and gravity from the original high sea cliffs which can be seen behind. At low tide Lannacombe is now a child's paradise with lots of rock pools and a lovely sandy stretch of beach.

East Prawle boasts two pubs and a village green. Just below the village is a National Trust car park and from here you can walk out to the coastal path and cliffs. This is one of the best places to spot the rare Cirl Bunting which nearly became extinct in this country. The Second World War gun emplacements were positioned to protect Salcombe Harbour and the top secret West Prawle Radar Station which was next to the village on the hill above.

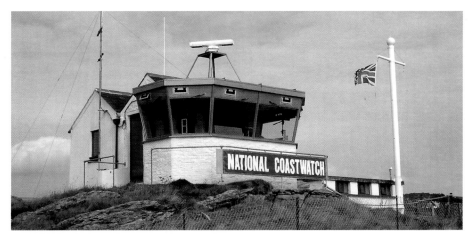

National Coast Watch at Prawle Point. Over the last twenty years the Coast Guard Service have closed most of their look-out stations as they pulled back to larger search and rescue operations centres as at Falmouth and Brixham. Their place has been taken by a charity organisation called National Coastwatch Institution. This organisation is now the eyes around our coast with a total of twenty three stations and they have a direct link with the main coast guard centres.

It takes a team of approximately fifty volunteers to keep the Coastwatch Station at Prawle Point operating 365 days a year. They not only keep an eye on vulnerable craft off the shore, they are also concerned with the safety of walkers using the cliff path.

In December 1992 the 9,800 ton coaster, 'Demetrios' was been towed in a force eleven severe storm from Dunkirk to the breaker's yard in Greece. Unfortunately the tow rope parted and the Demetrios ended up on the rocks below Prawle Point. The next day souvenir hunters put their lives at risk as they clambered over the wreck. As they staggered to the top of the cliff they were met by the police and asked to hand over their trophies as it all belonged to the Receiver of Wrecks.

A salvage team removed most of the steel plates from the hull but the costly operation sent the salvage company into liquidation. The picture shows all that is now left above the tide line.

These large pieces of slate, known as 'shiners', were used as ancient field boundaries throughout the area. These upright slate slabs are passed on the cliff path as it leaves Prawle Point.

Maceley Cove nestles under Gammon Head which is owned by the National Trust. Access to the beach is very steep and not for the faint hearted. It is a popular anchorage for pleasure craft out of Salcombe.

Decker's Cliffs near Gara Rock. The ancient field boundaries on the hillside above Deckler's Cliffs date back to the Bronze Age and Iron Age. There is also evidence of stone circles near the top of the hill. In 1857 an iron mine was worked on this site by the East Portlemouth Consolidated Mining Company. A tramway made its way down the seaward slope to a quay on Decker's Island, where the iron ore was loaded onto ships. The mining was abandoned in 1859 after a ship was wrecked while taking on the ore.

The Rickham Coast Guard Station, built about 1842, was sold by the Board of Trade to Richard Jordon and his family in 1909. It became a guest house and tea rooms and later renamed the Gara Rock Hotel which was so successful that in 1919 the original stone cottages were rendered and a second floor added. In 1940 the hotel was requisitioned by the RAF as headquarters and mess for officers and WRAF's serving with the West Prawle Radar Station. At the time of writing permission has been granted for the site's redevelopment.

Salcombe Estuary. On the eastern shores close to the mouth of Salcombe Estuary are the popular beaches of Sunny Cove and Mill Bay. There was a nine hole golf course on Portlemouth Downs, above the wooded area in the picture. It started during the 1920s and operated until the outbreak of war. Sadly it never reopened after the war.

During the Second World War, Mill Bay, Salcombe, was used as a military supply depot. It had a concrete ramp from the low water mark to the top of the beach for repairing the landing craft gathered in the harbour and preparing them for the D-Day invasion. It was finally demolished and removed in the late 1990s.

The Salcombe to East Portlemouth passenger ferry plies to and fro across the estuary in all weathers throughout the year.

Salcombe is a haven for sailing and has excellent moorings for both large and small craft. It also has a commercial fishing fleet and many of the old ship building yards still service the demand for nautical engineering and yacht maintenance.

The Salcombe Lifeboat disaster, 1916.

A small schooner, the 'Western Lass', had gone ashore in a furious gale just west of Start Point. The Salcombe lifeboat battled out through the wild seas across the bar to go to her aid. However, the schooner's crew had been saved by rocket lines from the shore, but the lifeboat crew only found this out when they arrived at the scene. Returning to Salcombe in the teeth of the gale was no easy task but the run in across the sand bar at the mouth of the estuary posed the greater risk. Streaming a drogue anchor and taking in all sail except her small mizzen the 'William and Emma' lined up for the run in. A monster wave caught her stern and made the lifeboat broach throwing all the crew over to one side, a second huge wave capsized the vessel pitching them into the stormy seas. Thirteen of the lifeboat's fifteen crew were drowned that day, a terrible blow to such a small seafaring community. Remarkably within a few months a new lifeboat and local crew were again venturing out to save seamen from the ravages of war and weather.

*Copies of this picture are available from the lifeboat shop and
all proceeds go towards the upkeep of Cliff House which
holds the original painting.*

33

Salcombe Life Boat Station now operates a Tyne Class, type 47-002 all weather lifeboat named Baltic Exchange II. It has a shallow conventional sheerline and flared bow above the waterline, with propellers protected by substantial bilge keels. It is constructed with a steel hull and aluminium superstructure which, when watertight, provides self righting ability. It can reach a speed of 17.5 knots with a range of 240 nautical miles. It is manned by a crew of six.

Since 2003 Salcombe has also operated an Atlantic 75 Inshore Lifeboat, B794 named Joan Bate. Even though her twin 70hp outboard engines make her one of the fastest lifeboats in the fleet, her hull design provides a softer ride than her predecessor for the three crew and anyone she may rescue.

Fort Charles and North Sands. Situated on a natural rock island near the mouth of the estuary between Salcombe town and North Sands, the fort was built in the 1540s as part of Henry VIII's coastal defence works. It was refortified in 1643-5 and re-named Fort Charles. During the Civil War it was one of the last strongholds of the Royalists but it finally surrendered to Parliamentary forces in 1646. It was dismantled in 1647. Later in the 18th or 19th century, a small watch tower was built onto the ruins of Fort Charles. The tower remains standing with the foundations of a bastion visible.

A ferry operates from North Sands to the centre of Salcombe. Passengers must first climb aboard a tractor driven platform which drives across the beach and into water deep enough for the ferry boat to pick them up.

Overbeck's Museum and Garden was given to the National Trust in 1937. It has a superb collection of insects and stuffed animals. The Maritime Room celebrates Salcombe's past as a prosperous port with paintings, photographs and models. There is even a secret room under the stairs full of children's toys.

The coastal path continues through the woods towards the dramatic scenery above Starehole Bay, where the Finish fore-masted barque 'Herzogin Cecilie' sank in 1936.